MANNERS MATTER TO MAEVIS

Maevis FOLLOWS THE RULES

Written by
Vicky Bureau
M.S., School Counseling

Illustrated by
Flavia Zuncheddu

A Starfish Book

SEAHORSE
PUBLISHING

T0020415

Teaching Tips for Caregivers:

As a caregiver, you can help your child succeed in school by giving them a strong foundation in language and literacy skills and a desire to learn to read.

This book helps children grow by letting them practice reading skills.

Reading for pleasure and interest will help your child to develop reading skills and will give your child the opportunity to practice these skills in meaningful ways.

- Encourage your child to read on her own at home
- Encourage your child to practice reading aloud
- Encourage activities that require reading
- Establish a reading time
- Talk with your child
- Give your child writing materials

Teaching Tips for Teachers:

Research shows that one of the best ways for students to learn a new topic is to read about it.

Before Reading

- Read the "Words to Know" and discuss the meaning of each word.
- Read the back cover to see what the book is about.

During Reading

- When a student gets to a word that is unknown, ask them to look at the rest of the sentence to find clues to help with the meaning of the unknown word.
- Ask the student to write down any pages of the book that were confusing to them.

After Reading

- Discuss the main idea of the book.
- Ask students to give one detail that they learned in the book by showing a text dependent answer from the book.

TABLE OF CONTENTS

Meet Maevis

This is Maevis.

School **manners** matter to Maevis.

School manners are the **rules** and **expectations** for learning.

Rules at School

In school, rules are what tell Maevis how to behave.

Maevis is expected to follow the rules.

Rules tell Maevis what she is allowed to do in school.

Rules also tell Maevis what she is not allowed to do in school.

Maevis Follows the Rules

Rules are **important** because they keep Maevis and her friends safe at school.

Rules help Maevis make good **decisions**.

11

School rules are also the same for everyone.

When rules are the same for everyone, they build expectations for how Maevis should behave.

In class, Maevis follows the classroom rules.

Maevis stays on task.

She raises her hand to talk.

At lunch, Maevis follows the cafeteria rules.

Maevis stays in her seat.

Maevis eats her lunch.

17

At recess, Maevis follows the playground rules.

Maevis keeps her hands to herself.

Maevis stays inside the playground area.

Rules tell Maevis what to do at school.

When Maevis doesn't know what to do, she can ask a grown-up.

Maevis wants to be safe in school.

And she wants to make good decisions.

That's why Maevis follows the rules!

WORDS TO KNOW

decisions (di-SIZH-uhnz): choices; the results of making up your mind

expectations (ek-spek-TAY-shuhnz): the rules that tell us what is okay to do and not to do

important (im-POR-tuhnt): something that matters a lot; having great meaning or value

manners (MAN-urs): the rules and expectations for learning; good behaviors

rules (roolz): official instructions or guidelines for behaviors and actions

INDEX

COMPREHENSION QUESTIONS

1. What are manners?

2. Name two ways Maevis uses manners at school.

3. Who should Maevis ask for help if she does not know what to do?

4. Why are rules important according to page 5?

ABOUT THE AUTHOR

Vicky Bureau was born in Longueuil, Quebec, and was raised in South Florida. As a teacher, she developed a passion for the social and emotional growth of her students and later transitioned into the area of child and adolescent psychology after earning her master's degree in school counseling.
In addition to working with children, Vicky loves to be surrounded by animals and nature. She lives in Fort Lauderdale with her family: Billy, Khloe, M.J., and Max; her three cats, Alley, Baguette, and Salem; and her dog, Boomer.

Written by: Vicky Bureau
Illustrated by: Flavia Zuncheddu
Design by: Under the Oaks Media
Editor: Kim Thompson

Library of Congress PCN Data
Maevis Follows the Rules / Vicky Bureau
Manners Matter to Maevis
ISBN 978-1-63897-459-8(hard cover)
ISBN 978-1-63897-574-8(paperback)
ISBN 978-1-63897-689-9(EPUB)
ISBN 978-1-63897-804-6(eBook)
Library of Congress Control Number: 2022932685

Printed in the United States of America.

Seahorse Publishing Company
www.seahorsepub.com

Published in the United States
Seahorse Publishing
PO Box 771325
Coral Springs, FL 33077